SLOW COOKER DOG FOOD COOKBOOK

Dr. Dashiell Mercer

1 SLOW COOKER DOG FOOD COOKBOOK

TABLE OF CONTENTS

INTRODUCTION

In the bustling world of veterinary clinics, where fur meets stethoscopes and wagging tails collide with compassionate hearts, I have been fortunate to witness countless stories of love and companionship between humans and their four-legged friends. Each appointment, each diagnosis, and each wagging tail carries with it a unique narrative—a tale of connection that resonates deep within us.

It was during one of those unforgettable moments that I first encountered the transformative power of a simple, yet profound idea—a concept that would forever change the way I approached the health and happiness of the animals entrusted to my care. Let me take you back to that moment, a moment that ignited a journey to craft a cookbook that would nourish both body and soul.

It was a chilly winter morning when Bailey, a senior Golden Retriever, and his owner, Mr. Anderson, walked through the doors of my clinic. As they took a seat, I could see the worry etched on Mr. Anderson's face and the slight limp in Bailey's step. Our examination revealed that Bailey's joints were feeling the toll of age, a common ailment among our senior companions.

As a veterinarian, my mission was clear: to provide the best care possible for Bailey. We discussed various treatment options, from medication to physical therapy, all designed to alleviate Bailey's discomfort. But it was a passing comment from Mr. Anderson that would send me down an unexpected path—one that would lead to the creation of a cookbook that would change lives.

Mr. Anderson shared his concern about Bailey's diet, worried that the commercial dog food he had been feeding him for years might not be providing the essential nutrients his aging body needed. As I listened to his worries, I was struck by a realization that would mark the beginning of a new chapter in my journey as a veterinarian.

I knew that nutrition played a pivotal role in a dog's overall health and well-being. But what if we could elevate the concept of pet nutrition beyond convenience and routine? What if we could infuse it with the same love and care that defined the relationship between a pet and their owner? That's when it hit me—a cookbook tailored to the unique dietary needs of our furry friends, prepared with the same devotion and thoughtfulness that Mr. Anderson had for Bailey.

As I delved deeper into the world of canine nutrition, I discovered the power of slow cooking. The gentle, slow simmering of ingredients not only retained their nutritional value but also unlocked Flavors that dogs savoured. It was as if slow cooking was a culinary love language that transcended the boundaries of species, allowing us to nourish our beloved companions in a way that resonated with their instincts and desires.

The journey that followed was marked by culinary exploration, trial and error, and heartwarming discoveries. I collaborated with nutritionists, chefs, and pet lovers to craft recipes that celebrated the diverse dietary requirements of our furry friends, from puppies bursting with youthful energy to seniors seeking comfort and support. Each recipe was a Labor of love—a testament to the bond we share with our pets and the lengths we are willing to go to ensure their well-being.

As I shared these slow-cooked creations with my patients and their families, I witnessed transformations that went beyond the physical. Dogs that once approached their bowls with indifference now eagerly devoured each bite. Their vitality and zest for life were rekindled, and the joy they brought to their families was immeasurable.

And so, the "Slow Cooker Dog Food Cookbook" was born—an ode to the power of love, nutrition, and the simple act of cooking with care. Within these pages, you'll find not only recipes but also stories—the stories of Bailey, of Mr. Anderson, and of countless others whose lives have been touched by the bond between a pet and their owner.

To my fellow veterinarians, I invite you to join me on this journey—a journey that has the potential to transform the way we approach pet care and nutrition. To pet owners, I offer you a culinary adventure that celebrates the joy of cooking for your furry companions and nourishing them with the love they deserve.

Welcome to a world where slow cooking is a bridge that connects our hearts with those of our pets—a world where the aroma of a simmering stew becomes a symphony of affection and wellness. Come, let us embark on a shared mission to nourish not only the bodies but also the spirits of our beloved companions, one recipe at a time.

CHAPTER 1

Slow Cooker Dog Food

In recent years, pet owners have been increasingly drawn to the idea of providing their furry companions with homemade meals, tailored to their specific nutritional needs. One method that has gained popularity in this Endeavor is the use of a slow cooker to prepare dog food. This method not only ensures that your dog's meals are packed with wholesome ingredients but also offers convenience and peace of mind for busy pet parents. In this guide, we will explore the benefits of homemade dog food, delve into the advantages of using a slow cooker for crafting canine cuisine, and provide essential safety tips and guidelines to ensure your pet's health and well-being.

Benefits of Homemade Dog Food

Nutritional Control: Crafting your own dog food enables you to have full control over the quality and variety of ingredients your furry friend consumes. You can customize meals to address specific dietary needs, allergies, or sensitivities, ensuring a well-balanced and nourishing diet.

Freshness and Quality: Homemade dog food allows you to use fresh, high-quality ingredients that may not be as readily available in commercial pet foods. This can lead to increased nutrient retention and a more palatable meal for your pup.

Avoiding Additives: Many commercial dog foods contain additives, preservatives, and artificial Flavors that might not align with your pet's health goals. By preparing meals at home, you can avoid these additives altogether.

Bonding and Care: Preparing food for your dog can strengthen the bond between you and your furry companion. It's an opportunity to show your care and love through the time and effort you invest in their well-being.

Using a Slow Cooker for Dog Meals

Gentle Cooking Process: Slow cookers operate at low temperatures over an extended period, which can help retain the nutritional value of ingredients while breaking down tougher cuts of meat and fibrous vegetables for easier digestion.

Flavour Infusion: The slow cooking process allows Flavors to meld together, creating a rich and enticing aroma that can make even the pickiest eaters excited for mealtime.

Convenience: Using a slow cooker simplifies the cooking process. Once the ingredients are in the pot, you can let the appliance do the work while you attend to other tasks.

Batch Cooking: Slow cookers are designed to accommodate larger quantities of food. This makes it convenient to prepare meals in bulk and store them for future use, reducing the time you spend in the kitchen.

Safety Tips and Guidelines

Balanced Diet: Consult your veterinarian or a veterinary nutritionist before making any dietary changes for your dog. Ensure that the recipes you prepare provide a well-balanced diet that meets their specific nutritional requirements.

Ingredient Awareness: Be aware of foods that are toxic to dogs, such as grapes, onions, garlic, and chocolate. Avoid including these ingredients in your homemade meals.

Cooking Times: While slow cooking is a safe method, make sure that meats, in particular, are cooked thoroughly to eliminate the risk of bacterial contamination.

Portion Control: Just like with commercial dog food, portion control is essential to prevent overfeeding or underfeeding. Your dog's age, size, and activity level should influence portion sizes.

Storage: Store any leftover dog food in airtight containers in the refrigerator or freezer to maintain freshness and prevent spoilage.

CHAPTER 2

Meaty Delights

1. Beef and Sweet Potato Stew

Cooking Time: 6 hours on low

Serving: About 4 cups

Ingredients:

- 1 lb lean ground beef
- 2 cups sweet potatoes peeled and cubed.
- 1 cup carrots, chopped.
- 1/2 cup peas
- 4 cups low-sodium beef broth
- 1 cup water
- 1 tablespoon olive oil

Instructions:

1. Cook the ground beef in a pan until it is browned. Drain the fat and transfer the beef to the slow cooker.
2. Add the sweet potatoes, carrots, and peas to the slow cooker.
3. Pour in the beef broth and water. Stir to combine all ingredients.
4. Cook for six hours on low with a cover.
5. Before serving, stir in the olive oil for added flavour.

Nutritional Information:

Calories: 300 per serving; Protein: 25g; Fat: 12g; Carbohydrates: 22g

2. Chicken and Rice Casserole

Cooking Time: 5 hours on low

Serving: About 3.5 cups

Ingredients:

- 2 boneless, skinless chicken breasts, diced.
- 1 cup brown rice
- 1/2 cup green beans, chopped.
- 1/2 cup carrots, diced.
- 2 cups low-sodium chicken broth
- 1 teaspoon dried parsley

Instructions:

1. Place the diced chicken, brown rice, green beans, and carrots in the slow cooker.
2. Pour the chicken broth over the ingredients and add dried parsley. Stir gently.
3. Cover and cook on low for 5 hours.
4. Once cooked, let it cool before serving to your furry friend.

Nutritional Information:

Calories: 280 per serving; Protein: 20g; Fat: 5g; Carbohydrates: 40g

3. Turkey and Pumpkin Stew

Cooking Time: 4.5 hours on low

Serving: About 3 cups

Ingredients:

- 1 lb ground turkey
- 1 cup pumpkin puree (unsweetened)
- 1/2 cup spinach, chopped.
- 1/2 cup peas
- 3 cups low-sodium turkey or chicken broth
- 1 tablespoon coconut oil

Instructions:

1. Brown the ground turkey in a skillet and transfer it to the slow cooker.
2. Add the pumpkin puree, chopped spinach, and peas to the slow cooker.
3. Pour in the turkey or chicken broth. Mix well.
4. Cover and cook on low for 4.5 hours.
5. Just before serving, stir in the coconut oil.

Nutritional Information:

Calories: 240 per serving; Protein: 18g; Fat: 10g; Carbohydrates: 18g

4. Pork and Barley Stew

Cooking Time: 6 hours on low

Serving: About 4 cups

Ingredients:

- 1 lb pork loin, cubed.
- 1 cup barley
- 1/2 cup carrots, sliced.
- 1/2 cup green peas
- 4 cups low-sodium pork or vegetable broth

Instructions:

1. Place the pork cubes, barley, sliced carrots, and green peas in the slow cooker.
2. Pour in the pork or vegetable broth.
3. Stir gently to combine all the ingredients.
4. Cover and cook on low for 6 hours.

Nutritional Information:

Calories: 320 per serving; Protein: 22g; Fat: 10g; Carbohydrates: 34g

5. Salmon and Quinoa Delight

Cooking Time: 4 hours on low

Serving: About 3.5 cups

Ingredients:

- 1 cup salmon fillet cooked and flaked.
- 1 cup quinoa, rinsed.
- 1/2 cup sweet potatoes, diced.
- 1/2 cup broccoli florets
- 2 cups low-sodium fish or vegetable broth

Instructions:

1. In the slow cooker, combine the cooked and flaked salmon, quinoa, diced sweet potatoes, and broccoli florets.
2. Pour in the fish or vegetable broth.
3. Gently mix the ingredients together.
4. Cover and cook on low for 4 hours.

Nutritional Information:

Calories: 280 per serving; Protein: 20g; Fat: 7g; Carbohydrates: 30g

6. Lamb and Lentil Stew

Cooking Time: 5.5 hours on low

Serving: About 3.5 cups

Ingredients:

- 1 lb ground lamb
- 1 cup brown lentils, rinsed.
- 1/2 cup carrots, chopped.
- 1/2 cup zucchini, diced.
- 3 cups low-sodium lamb or vegetable broth

Instructions:

1. Brown the ground lamb in a skillet and transfer it to the slow cooker.
2. Add the brown lentils, chopped carrots, and diced zucchini to the slow cooker.
3. Pour in the lamb or vegetable broth. Mix well.
4. Cover and cook on low for 5.5 hours.

Nutritional Information:

Calories: 300 per serving; Protein: 18g; Fat: 12g; Carbohydrates: 30g

7. Turkey and Cranberry Stew

Cooking Time: 4 hours on low

Serving: About 3 cups

Ingredients:

- 1 lb ground turkey
- 1 cup cooked quinoa
- 1/4 cup cranberries, fresh or frozen
- 1/2 cup green beans, chopped.
- 2 cups low-sodium turkey or chicken broth

Instructions:

1. Brown the ground turkey in a skillet and transfer it to the slow cooker.
2. Add the cooked quinoa, cranberries, and chopped green beans to the slow cooker.
3. Pour in the turkey or chicken broth. Mix well.
4. Cover and cook on low for 4 hours.

Nutritional Information:

Calories: 260 per serving; Protein: 18g; Fat: 8g; Carbohydrates: 28g

CHAPTER 3

Wholesome Grain and Veggie Mixes

8. Brown Rice and Veggie Medley

Cooking Time: 4 hours on low

Serving: About 3 cups

Ingredients:

- 1 cup cooked brown rice.
- 1 cup mixed vegetables (carrots, peas, green beans), chopped.
- 1/2 cup pumpkin puree (unsweetened)
- 2 cups low-sodium vegetable broth

Instructions:

1. Combine cooked brown rice, chopped mixed vegetables, and pumpkin puree in the slow cooker.
2. Pour in the vegetable broth and mix well.
3. Cook for 4 hours on low with a cover.

Nutritional Information:

Calories: 180 per serving; Protein: 4g; Fat: 1g; Carbohydrates: 40g

9. Chicken and Quinoa Garden Blend

Cooking Time: 5 hours on low

Serving: About 3.5 cups

Ingredients:

- 1 cup cooked quinoa
- 1 cup boneless, skinless chicken breast, diced.
- 1/2 cup carrots, diced.
- 1/2 cup zucchini, chopped.
- 2 cups low-sodium chicken broth

Instructions:

1. Combine cooked quinoa, diced chicken breast, diced carrots, and chopped zucchini in the slow cooker.
2. Pour in the chicken broth and mix well.
3. Cover and cook on low for 5 hours.

Nutritional Information:

Calories: 220 per serving; Protein: 18g; Fat: 2g; Carbohydrates: 35g

10. Barley and Mixed Greens Delight

Cooking Time: 4.5 hours on low

Serving: About 3 cups

Ingredients:

- 1 cup cooked barley
- 1 cup mixed leafy greens (kale, spinach, collard greens), chopped.
- 1/2 cup blueberries
- 2 cups low-sodium vegetable broth

Instructions:

1. Combine cooked barley, chopped mixed greens, and blueberries in the slow cooker.
2. Pour in the vegetable broth and mix well.
3. Cover and cook on low for 4.5 hours.

Nutritional Information:

Calories: 160 per serving; Protein: 3g; Fat: 1g; Carbohydrates: 35g

11. Beef and Brown Rice Harmony

Cooking Time: 6 hours on low

Serving: About 4 cups

Ingredients:

- 1 cup cooked brown rice.
- 1 cup lean ground beef
- 1/2 cup sweet potatoes, diced.
- 1/2 cup broccoli florets
- 2 cups low-sodium beef broth

Instructions:

1. Brown the lean ground beef in a skillet and transfer it to the slow cooker.
2. Add cooked brown rice, diced sweet potatoes, and broccoli florets to the slow cooker.
3. Pour in the beef broth and mix well.
4. Cover and cook on low for 6 hours.

Nutritional Information:

Calories: 240 per serving; Protein: 15g; Fat: 8g; Carbohydrates: 30g

12.   Salmon and Mixed Veggies Medley

Cooking Time: 4 hours on low

Serving: About 3.5 cups

Ingredients:

- 1 cup cooked quinoa
- 1 cup cooked salmon, flaked.
- 1/2 cup mixed vegetables (carrots, peas, green beans), chopped.
- 2 cups low-sodium fish or vegetable broth

Instructions:

1. Combine cooked quinoa, flaked salmon, and chopped mixed vegetables in the slow cooker.
2. Pour in the fish or vegetable broth and mix well.
3. Cover and cook on low for 4 hours.

Nutritional Information:

Calories: 260 per serving; Protein: 20g; Fat: 6g; Carbohydrates: 30g

13.   Turkey and Potato Harmony

Cooking Time: 5 hours on low

Serving: About 3.5 cups

Ingredients:

- 1 cup cooked sweet potatoes, diced.
- 1 cup cooked quinoa
- 1/2 cup ground turkey
- 1/2 cup green peas
- 2 cups low-sodium turkey or chicken broth

Instructions:

1. Brown the ground turkey in a skillet and transfer it to the slow cooker.
2. Add cooked sweet potatoes, cooked quinoa, and green peas to the slow cooker.
3. Pour in the turkey or chicken broth and mix well.
4. Cover and cook on low for 5 hours.

Nutritional Information:

Calories: 230 per serving; Protein: 16g; Fat: 4g; Carbohydrates: 35g

CHAPTER 4

Pawsitively Delicious Stews

14.   Chicken and Sweet Potato Stew

Cooking Time: 4 hours on low

Serving: About 3 cups

Ingredients:

- 1 cup cooked chicken breast, shredded.
- 1 cup sweet potatoes, diced.
- 1/2 cup carrots, chopped.
- 1/2 cup green beans, chopped.
- 2 cups low-sodium chicken broth

Instructions:

1. Combine shredded chicken breast, diced sweet potatoes, chopped carrots, and chopped green beans in the slow cooker.
2. Pour in the chicken broth and mix well.
3. Cover and cook on low for 4 hours.

Nutritional Information:

Calories: 220 per serving; Protein: 20g; Fat: 2g; Carbohydrates: 30g

15.   Beef and Pumpkin Stew

Cooking Time: 5 hours on low

Serving: About 3.5 cups

Ingredients:

- 1 cup lean ground beef
- 1 cup pumpkin puree (unsweetened)
- 1/2 cup peas
- 1/2 cup carrots, diced.
- 2 cups low-sodium beef broth

Instructions:

1. Brown the lean ground beef in a skillet and transfer it to the slow cooker.
2. Add pumpkin puree, peas, and diced carrots to the slow cooker.
3. Pour in the beef broth and mix well.
4. Cover and cook on low for 5 hours.

Nutritional Information:

Calories: 230 per serving; Protein: 18g; Fat: 8g; Carbohydrates: 30g

16. Turkey and Spinach Delight

Cooking Time: 4.5 hours on low

Serving: About 3 cups

Ingredients:

- 1 cup cooked ground turkey
- 1 cup spinach, chopped.
- 1/2 cup carrots, diced.
- 1/2 cup quinoa, cooked.
- 2 cups low-sodium turkey or chicken broth

Instructions:

1. Combine cooked ground turkey, chopped spinach, diced carrots, and cooked quinoa in the slow cooker.
2. Pour in the turkey or chicken broth and mix well.
3. Cover and cook on low for 4.5 hours.

Nutritional Information:

Calories: 220 per serving; Protein: 18g; Fat: 6g; Carbohydrates: 28g

17. Lamb and Brown Rice Medley

Cooking Time: 6 hours on low

Serving: About 4 cups

Ingredients:

- 1 cup cooked ground lamb
- 1 cup cooked brown rice.
- 1/2 cup green peas
- 1/2 cup sweet potatoes, diced.
- 2 cups low-sodium lamb or vegetable broth

Instructions:

1. Combine cooked ground lamb, cooked brown rice, green peas, and diced sweet potatoes in the slow cooker.
2. Pour in the lamb or vegetable broth and mix well.
3. Cover and cook on low for 6 hours.

Nutritional Information:

Calories: 260 per serving; Protein: 18g; Fat: 8g; Carbohydrates: 30g

18.   Salmon and Carrot Stew

Cooking Time: 4 hours on low

Serving: About 3.5 cups

Ingredients:

- 1 cup cooked salmon, flaked.
- 1 cup carrots, diced.
- 1/2 cup peas
- 1/2 cup cooked quinoa
- 2 cups low-sodium fish or vegetable broth

Instructions:

1. Combine cooked salmon, diced carrots, peas, and cooked quinoa in the slow cooker.
2. Pour in the fish or vegetable broth and mix well.
3. Cover and cook on low for 4 hours.

Nutritional Information:

Calories: 240 per serving; Protein: 20g; Fat: 6g; Carbohydrates: 30g

19. Pork and Mixed Veggie Stew

Cooking Time: 5.5 hours on low

Serving: About 3.5 cups

Ingredients:

- 1 cup cooked lean ground pork.
- 1 cup mixed vegetables (carrots, peas, green beans), chopped.
- 1/2 cup sweet potatoes, diced.
- 1/2 cup barley, cooked.
- 2 cups low-sodium vegetable broth

Instructions:

1. Combine cooked lean ground pork, chopped mixed vegetables, diced sweet potatoes, and cooked barley in the slow cooker.
2. Pour in the vegetable broth and mix well.
3. Cover and cook on low for 5.5 hours.

Nutritional Information:

Calories: 240 per serving; Protein: 18g; Fat: 6g; Carbohydrates: 32g

20. Veggie and Lentil Delight

Cooking Time: 4 hours on low

Serving: About 3 cups

Ingredients:

- 1 cup mixed vegetables (carrots, peas, green beans), chopped.
- 1/2 cup brown lentils, rinsed.
- 1/2 cup sweet potatoes, diced.
- 1/2 cup spinach, chopped.
- 2 cups low-sodium vegetable broth

Instructions:

1. Combine chopped mixed vegetables, rinsed brown lentils, diced sweet potatoes, and chopped spinach in the slow cooker.
2. Pour in the vegetable broth and mix well.
3. Cover and cook on low for 4 hours.

Nutritional Information:

Calories: 180 per serving; Protein: 8g; Fat: 1g; Carbohydrates: 35g

CHAPTER 5

Treats and Snacks

21. Peanut Butter Pumpkin Bites

Cooking Time: 2 hours on low

Serving: About 20 small bites

Ingredients:

- 1 cup pumpkin puree (unsweetened)
- 1/2 cup natural peanut butter (unsalted)
- 1 cup whole wheat flour

Instructions:

1. In a bowl, mix pumpkin puree and peanut butter until well combined.
2. Gradually add whole wheat flour and knead the mixture into a dough.
3. Roll small portions of the dough into bite-sized balls.
4. Place the balls in the slow cooker and cook on low for 2 hours.

Nutritional Information:

Calories: 30 per bite; Protein: 1g; Fat: 1.5g; Carbohydrates: 3g

22. Banana Oat Delights

Cooking Time: 2.5 hours on low

Serving: About 15 small treats

Ingredients:

- 2 ripe bananas, mashed.
- 1 cup rolled oats.
- 1/4 cup unsweetened applesauce

Instructions:

1. In a bowl, combine mashed bananas, rolled oats, and applesauce.
2. Form small, flat treats, and place them in the slow cooker.
3. Cook on low for 2.5 hours.

Nutritional Information:

Calories: 25 per treat; Protein: 0.5g; Fat: 0.5g; Carbohydrates: 5g

23. Cheesy Sweet Potato Biscuits

Cooking Time: 2.5 hours on low

Serving: About 20 small biscuits

Ingredients:

- 1 cup cooked sweet potatoes, mashed.
- 1/2 cup shredded cheddar cheese
- 1 cup brown rice flour

Instructions:

1. In a bowl, mix mashed sweet potatoes and shredded cheddar cheese.
2. Gradually add brown rice flour and knead the mixture into a dough.
3. Roll out the dough and use a cookie cutter to shape biscuits.
4. Place the biscuits in the slow cooker and cook on low for 2.5 hours.

Nutritional Information:

Calories: 40 per biscuit; Protein: 1.5g; Fat: 1.5g; Carbohydrates: 6g

24.   Chicken and Carrot Crunchies

Cooking Time: 3 hours on low

Serving: About 30 small treats

Ingredients:

- 1 cup cooked chicken breast, shredded.
- 1/2 cup carrot, grated.
- 1 cup oat flour

Instructions:

1. In a bowl, combine shredded chicken breast and grated carrot.
2. Gradually add oat flour and mix until a dough forms.
3. Roll small portions of the dough into bite-sized treats.
4. Place the treats in the slow cooker and cook on low for 3 hours.

Nutritional Information:

Calories: 20 per treat; Protein: 1g; Fat: 0.5g; Carbohydrates: 3g

25. Apple Cinnamon Bites

Cooking Time: 2 hours on low

Serving: About 25 small bites

Ingredients:

- 1 cup unsweetened applesauce
- 1 cup oat flour
- 1/2 teaspoon cinnamon

Instructions:

1. In a bowl, mix unsweetened applesauce and oat flour until combined.
2. Add cinnamon and mix thoroughly.
3. Roll the mixture into small balls and place them in the slow cooker.
4. Cook on low for 2 hours.

Nutritional Information:

Calories: 15 per bite; Protein: 0.5g; Fat: 0.5g; Carbohydrates: 3g

26. Blueberry Coconut Bites

Cooking Time: 2 hours on low

Serving: About 20 small bites

Ingredients:

- 1/2 cup blueberries, mashed
- 1/2 cup coconut flour
- 1 egg

Instructions:

1. In a bowl, combine mashed blueberries, coconut flour, and egg.
2. Mix until a dough forms.
3. Roll small portions of the dough into bite-sized balls.
4. Place the balls in the slow cooker and cook on low for 2 hours.

Nutritional Information:

Calories: 25 per bite; Protein: 1g; Fat: 1g; Carbohydrates: 4g

27. Pumpkin Peanut Butter Drops

Cooking Time: 2.5 hours on low

Serving: About 25 small drops

Ingredients:

- 1/2 cup pumpkin puree (unsweetened)
- 1/2 cup natural peanut butter (unsalted)
- 1/2 cup oat flour

Instructions:

1. In a bowl, mix pumpkin puree and peanut butter until well combined.
2. Gradually add oat flour and mix until a dough forms.
3. Drop small spoonful of the dough onto a baking sheet and place it in the slow cooker.
4. Cook on low for 2.5 hours.

Nutritional Information:

Calories: 30 per drop; Protein: 1g; Fat: 2g; Carbohydrates: 2g

28. Carrot and Parsley Crunchies

Cooking Time: 3 hours on low

Serving: About 30 small treats

Ingredients:

- 1 cup carrot, grated.
- 1/2 cup fresh parsley, chopped.
- 1 cup rice flour

Instructions:

1. In a bowl, combine grated carrot and chopped parsley.
2. Gradually add rice flour and knead until a dough forms.
3. Roll small portions of the dough into bite-sized treats.
4. Place the treats in the slow cooker and cook on low for 3 hours.

Nutritional Information:

Calories: 15 per treat; Protein: 0.5g; Fat: 0g; Carbohydrates: 3g

29.   Turkey and Cranberry Biscuits

Cooking Time: 2.5 hours on low

Serving: About 20 small biscuits

Ingredients:

- 1 cup cooked ground turkey
- 1/4 cup dried cranberries (unsweetened)
- 1 cup oat flour

Instructions:

1. In a bowl, combine cooked ground turkey and dried cranberries.
2. Gradually add oat flour and knead the mixture into a dough.
3. Roll out the dough and use a cookie cutter to shape biscuits.
4. Place the biscuits in the slow cooker and cook on low for 2.5 hours.

Nutritional Information:

Calories: 30 per biscuit; Protein: 2g; Fat: 1g; Carbohydrates: 3g

30. Spinach and Cheese Bites

Cooking Time: 2 hours on low

Serving: About 20 small bites

Ingredients:

- 1/2 cup cooked spinach, chopped.
- 1/2 cup shredded cheddar cheese
- 1/2 cup oat flour

Instructions:

1. In a bowl, combine chopped cooked spinach and shredded cheddar cheese.
2. Gradually add oat flour and mix until a dough forms.
3. Roll small portions of the dough into bite-sized balls.
4. Place the balls in the slow cooker and cook on low for 2 hours.

Nutritional Information:

Calories: 25 per bite; Protein: 1g; Fat: 1.5g; Carbohydrates: 2g

CHAPTER 6

Special Diets for Dogs with Dietary Restrictions

31.   Grain-Free Turkey and Veggie Stew

Cooking Time: 4 hours on low

Serving: About 3 cups

Ingredients:

- 1 cup ground turkey
- 1/2 cup zucchini, diced.
- 1/2 cup carrots, chopped.
- 1/2 cup green beans, chopped.
- 2 cups low-sodium turkey or vegetable broth

Instructions:

1. Brown the ground turkey in a skillet and transfer it to the slow cooker.
2. Add diced zucchini, chopped carrots, and chopped green beans to the slow cooker.
3. Pour in the turkey or vegetable broth and mix well.
4. Cover and cook on low for 4 hours.

Nutritional Information:

Calories: 220 per serving; Protein: 18g; Fat: 8g; Carbohydrates: 20g

32.   Limited Ingredient Chicken and Rice Stew

Cooking Time: 5 hours on low

Serving: About 3.5 cups

Ingredients:

- 1 cup cooked chicken breast, shredded.
- 1 cup white rice, cooked.
- 1/2 cup pumpkin puree (unsweetened)
- 1/2 cup carrots, diced.
- 2 cups low-sodium chicken broth

Instructions:

1. Combine shredded chicken breast, cooked white rice, pumpkin puree, and diced carrots in the slow cooker.
2. Pour in the chicken broth and mix well.
3. Cover and cook on low for 5 hours.

Nutritional Information:

Calories: 200 per serving; Protein: 16g; Fat: 2g; Carbohydrates: 28g

33. Low-Fat Turkey and Rice Medley

Cooking Time: 4.5 hours on low

Serving: About 3 cups

Ingredients:

- 1 cup lean ground turkey
- 1/2 cup cooked brown rice.
- 1/2 cup green beans, chopped.
- 1/2 cup carrots, diced.
- 2 cups low-sodium turkey or vegetable broth

Instructions:

1. Brown the lean ground turkey in a skillet and transfer it to the slow cooker.
2. Add cooked brown rice, chopped green beans, and diced carrots to the slow cooker.
3. Pour in the turkey or vegetable broth and mix well.
4. Cover and cook on low for 4.5 hours.

Nutritional Information:

Calories: 180 per serving; Protein: 14g; Fat: 4g; Carbohydrates: 20g

34. Sensitive Stomach Chicken and Pumpkin Stew

Cooking Time: 5 hours on low

Serving: About 3.5 cups

Ingredients:

- 1 cup cooked chicken breast, shredded.

- 1 cup pumpkin puree (unsweetened)

- 1/2 cup cooked quinoa

- 1/2 cup green beans, chopped.

- 2 cups low-sodium chicken or vegetable broth

Instructions:

1. Combine shredded chicken breast, pumpkin puree, cooked quinoa, and chopped green beans in the slow cooker.

2. Pour in the chicken or vegetable broth and mix well.

3. Cover and cook on low for 5 hours.

Nutritional Information:

Calories: 180 per serving; Protein: 14g; Fat: 2g; Carbohydrates: 26g

35.   Limited Ingredient Lamb and Sweet Potato Stew

Cooking Time: 4 hours on low

Serving: About 3 cups

Ingredients:

- 1 cup ground lamb
- 1/2 cup sweet potatoes, diced.
- 1/2 cup green peas
- 1/2 cup butternut squash, diced.
- 2 cups low-sodium lamb or vegetable broth

Instructions:

1. Brown the ground lamb in a skillet and transfer it to the slow cooker.
2. Add diced sweet potatoes, green peas, and diced butternut squash to the slow cooker.
3. Pour in the lamb or vegetable broth and mix well.
4. Cover and cook on low for 4 hours.

Nutritional Information:

Calories: 210 per serving; Protein: 16g; Fat: 8g; Carbohydrates: 18g

36. Low-Phosphorus Chicken and Rice Stew (Kidney-Friendly)

Cooking Time: 5 hours on low

Serving: About 3.5 cups

Ingredients:

- 1 cup cooked chicken breast, shredded.
- 1 cup white rice, cooked.
- 1/2 cup zucchini, diced.
- 1/2 cup carrots, chopped.
- 2 cups low-sodium chicken or vegetable broth

Instructions:

1. Combine shredded chicken breast, cooked white rice, diced zucchini, and chopped carrots in the slow cooker.
2. Pour in the chicken or vegetable broth and mix well.
3. Cover and cook on low for 5 hours.

Nutritional Information:

Calories: 220 per serving; Protein: 16g; Fat: 2g; Carbohydrates: 32g

37. Hypoallergenic Turkey and Potato Stew

Cooking Time: 4 hours on low

Serving: About 3 cups

Ingredients:

- 1 cup ground turkey
- 1/2 cup potatoes, diced.
- 1/2 cup green beans, chopped.
- 1/2 cup carrots, chopped.
- 2 cups low-sodium turkey or vegetable broth

Instructions:

1. Brown the ground turkey in a skillet and transfer it to the slow cooker.
2. Add diced potatoes, chopped green beans, and chopped carrots to the slow cooker.
3. Pour in the turkey or vegetable broth and mix well.
4. Cover and cook on low for 4 hours.

Nutritional Information:

Calories: 200 per serving; Protein: 18g; Fat: 6g; Carbohydrates: 18g

38.   Weight Management Chicken and Pumpkin Stew

Cooking Time: 5 hours on low

Serving: About 3.5 cups

Ingredients:

- 1 cup cooked chicken breast, shredded.
- 1 cup pumpkin puree (unsweetened)
- 1/2 cup green beans, chopped.
- 1/2 cup carrots, chopped.
- 2 cups low-sodium chicken or vegetable broth

Instructions:

1. Combine shredded chicken breast, pumpkin puree, chopped green beans, and chopped carrots in the slow cooker.
2. Pour in the chicken or vegetable broth and mix well.
3. Cover and cook on low for 5 hours.

Nutritional Information:

Calories: 160 per serving; Protein: 14g; Fat: 1g; Carbohydrates: 26g

39. Low-Carbohydrate Beef and Broccoli Stew

Cooking Time: 4 hours on low

Serving: About 3 cups

Ingredients:

- 1 cup lean ground beef
- 1/2 cup broccoli florets
- 1/2 cup zucchini, diced.
- 1/2 cup cauliflower, chopped.
- 2 cups low-sodium beef or vegetable broth

Instructions:

1. Brown the lean ground beef in a skillet and transfer it to the slow cooker.
2. Add broccoli florets, diced zucchini, and chopped cauliflower to the slow cooker.
3. Pour in the beef or vegetable broth and mix well.
4. Cover and cook on low for 4 hours.

Nutritional Information:

Calories: 220 per serving; Protein: 18g; Fat: 8g; Carbohydrates: 10g

40.　High-Fiber Chicken and Pumpkin Stew (Digestive Health)

Cooking Time: 4.5 hours on low

Serving: About 3 cups

Ingredients:

- 1 cup cooked chicken breast, shredded.
- 1 cup pumpkin puree (unsweetened)
- 1/2 cup sweet potatoes, diced.
- 1/2 cup green peas
- 2 cups low-sodium chicken or vegetable broth

Instructions:

1. Combine shredded chicken breast, pumpkin puree, diced sweet potatoes, and green peas in the slow cooker.
2. Pour in the chicken or vegetable broth and mix well.
3. Cover and cook on low for 4.5 hours.

Nutritional Information:

Calories: 190 per serving; Protein: 16g; Fat: 1.5g; Carbohydrates: 30g

CHAPTER 7

Senior and Puppy Meals

41. Senior Chicken and Rice Stew

Cooking Time: 4 hours on low

Serving: About 3 cups

Ingredients:

- 1 cup cooked chicken breast, shredded.
- 1/2 cup brown rice, cooked.
- 1/2 cup sweet potatoes, diced.
- 1/2 cup carrots, chopped.
- 2 cups low-sodium chicken or vegetable broth

Instructions:

1. Combine shredded chicken breast, cooked brown rice, diced sweet potatoes, and chopped carrots in the slow cooker.
2. Pour in the chicken or vegetable broth and mix well.
3. Cover and cook on low for 4 hours.

Nutritional Information:

Calories: 200 per serving; Protein: 16g; Fat: 2g; Carbohydrates: 28g

42. Puppy Turkey and Pumpkin Stew

Cooking Time: 5 hours on low

Serving: About 3.5 cups

Ingredients:

- 1 cup ground turkey
- 1/2 cup pumpkin puree (unsweetened)
- 1/2 cup sweet potatoes, diced
- 1/2 cup peas
- 2 cups low-sodium turkey or vegetable broth

Instructions:

1. Brown the ground turkey in a skillet and transfer it to the slow cooker.
2. Add pumpkin puree, diced sweet potatoes, and peas to the slow cooker.
3. Pour in the turkey or vegetable broth and mix well.
4. Cover and cook on low for 5 hours.

Nutritional Information:

Calories: 220 per serving; Protein: 18g; Fat: 4g; Carbohydrates: 26g

43. Senior Salmon and Quinoa Medley

Cooking Time: 4.5 hours on low

Serving: About 3 cups

Ingredients:

- 1 cup cooked salmon, flaked.
- 1/2 cup cooked quinoa
- 1/2 cup carrots, diced.
- 1/2 cup peas
- 2 cups low-sodium fish or vegetable broth

Instructions:

1. Combine flaked salmon, cooked quinoa, diced carrots, and peas in the slow cooker.
2. Pour in the fish or vegetable broth and mix well.
3. Cover and cook on low for 4.5 hours.

Nutritional Information:

Calories: 220 per serving; Protein: 18g; Fat: 6g; Carbohydrates: 28g

44. Puppy Chicken and Oat Stew

Cooking Time: 5 hours on low

Serving: About 3.5 cups

Ingredients:

- 1 cup cooked chicken breast, shredded.
- 1/2 cup oats
- 1/2 cup green beans, chopped.
- 1/2 cup carrots, chopped.
- 2 cups low-sodium chicken or vegetable broth

Instructions:

1. Combine shredded chicken breast, oats, chopped green beans, and chopped carrots in the slow cooker.
2. Pour in the chicken or vegetable broth and mix well.
3. Cover and cook on low for 5 hours.

Nutritional Information:

Calories: 180 per serving; Protein: 16g; Fat: 2g; Carbohydrates: 24g

45. Senior Beef and Potato Stew

Cooking Time: 4 hours on low

Serving: About 3 cups

Ingredients:

- 1 cup lean ground beef
- 1/2 cup potatoes, diced.
- 1/2 cup green peas
- 1/2 cup carrots, diced.
- 2 cups low-sodium beef or vegetable broth

Instructions:

1. Brown the lean ground beef in a skillet and transfer it to the slow cooker.
2. Add diced potatoes, green peas, and diced carrots to the slow cooker.
3. Pour in the beef or vegetable broth and mix well.
4. Cover and cook on low for 4 hours.

Nutritional Information:

Calories: 200 per serving; Protein: 16g; Fat: 6g; Carbohydrates: 20g

46. Puppy Turkey and Sweet Potato Stew

Cooking Time: 5 hours on low

Serving: About 3.5 cups

Ingredients:

- 1 cup ground turkey
- 1/2 cup sweet potatoes, diced.
- 1/2 cup green beans, chopped.
- 1/2 cup carrots, chopped.
- 2 cups low-sodium turkey or vegetable broth

Instructions:

1. Brown the ground turkey in a skillet and transfer it to the slow cooker.
2. Add diced sweet potatoes, chopped green beans, and chopped carrots to the slow cooker.
3. Pour in the turkey or vegetable broth and mix well.
4. Cover and cook on low for 5 hours.

Nutritional Information:

Calories: 220 per serving; Protein: 18g; Fat: 4g; Carbohydrates: 26g

CHAPTER 8

28 Day Meal Plan

Day	Breakfast	Lunch	Dinner
1	Chicken and Rice	Turkey and Sweet Potato	Beef and Vegetable Stew
2	Oatmeal with Blueberries	Salmon and Quinoa Medley	Chicken and Rice
3	Pumpkin and Cottage Cheese	Green Bean and Chicken Mix	Turkey and Pumpkin Stew
4	Scrambled Eggs	Ground Beef with Carrots	Quinoa and Spinach Surprise
5	Yogurt and Banana	Turkey and Rice	Lamb and Sweet Potato Stew
6	Chicken and Sweet Potato	Pumpkin and Turkey	Oatmeal with Berries
7	Rice and Ground Beef	Chicken and Broccoli Mix	Salmon and Vegetable Medley
8	Cottage Cheese with Berries	Beef and Potato	Chicken and Rice
9	Quinoa and Carrot Mix	Turkey and Spinach Surprise	Beef and Vegetable Stew
10	Omelette with Vegetables	Chicken and Rice	Pumpkin and Cottage Cheese

11	Turkey and Pumpkin Stew	Salmon and Quinoa Medley	Chicken and Sweet Potato
12	Rice and Green Beans	Beef and Vegetable Stew	Oatmeal with Blueberries
13	Chicken and Broccoli Mix	Lamb and Sweet Potato Stew	Turkey and Rice
14	Scrambled Eggs with Spinach	Ground Beef with Carrots	Pumpkin and Turkey
15	Cottage Cheese with Carrots	Chicken and Rice	Salmon and Vegetable Medley
16	Quinoa and Spinach Surprise	Turkey and Spinach Surprise	Beef and Potato
17	Yogurt and Berries	Beef and Vegetable Stew	Chicken and Sweet Potato
18	Chicken and Rice	Turkey and Rice	Oatmeal with Berries
19	Pumpkin and Turkey	Chicken and Broccoli Mix	Salmon and Quinoa Medley
20	Rice and Ground Beef	Beef and Vegetable Stew	Turkey and Pumpkin Stew
21	Scrambled Eggs	Lamb and Sweet Potato Stew	Chicken and Rice
22	Cottage Cheese with Spinach	Pumpkin and Cottage Cheese	Beef and Vegetable Stew
23	Oatmeal with Banana	Ground Beef with Carrots	Salmon and Vegetable Medley
24	Chicken and Sweet Potato	Turkey and Spinach Surprise	Quinoa and Carrot Mix

25	Rice and Green Beans	Chicken and Rice	Lamb and Sweet Potato Stew
26	Turkey and Pumpkin Stew	Beef and Potato	Chicken and Broccoli Mix
27	Yogurt and Blueberries	Salmon and Quinoa Medley	Pumpkin and Turkey
28	Chicken and Rice	Beef and Vegetable Stew	Oatmeal with Berries

CONCLUSION

In closing, I want to express my sincere gratitude for joining us on this culinary journey through the realm of slow cooker dog food. As we bid farewell to these pages filled with recipes designed to nourish and delight our furry companions, I hope you've discovered the artistry and love that go into crafting meals that truly speak to the hearts of our dogs.

Throughout this cookbook, we've ventured into kitchens where the aroma of simmering stews and the sizzle of savory treats have filled the air. We've learned that the act of cooking for our dogs goes beyond mere sustenance; it's a way of forging a deeper connection with our loyal companions and showing them how much they mean to us.

As you embark on your own culinary odyssey, experimenting with flavors, textures, and ingredients, I invite you to savor not only the delightful results but also the shared moments of anticipation and joy that come with mealtime. There's a special kind of magic that happens when we watch our dogs relishing the dishes we've prepared with care and devotion.

Your thoughts and experiences are incredibly valuable to us. We would be honored if you could take a moment to leave a review of this cookbook, sharing your insights, stories, and even your dog's reactions to the recipes. Your feedback will not only help us improve and refine our offerings but will also guide fellow dog lovers in choosing the perfect recipes for their four-legged companions.

Leaving a review is a way of extending the journey we've taken together, building a community of passionate individuals who are dedicated to providing the best for their dogs. Your words have the power to inspire and guide others on their own culinary adventures, ensuring that the bond between humans and their furry friends continues to thrive.

In a world that moves swiftly, our dogs remain steadfast companions, offering us unconditional love and unwavering loyalty. By cooking for them with intention and affection, we're not just nourishing their bodies—we're nurturing the very essence of our relationship with them.

From our kitchen to yours, we thank you for allowing us to be a part of your dog's journey toward health, happiness, and full bellies. Your review will echo through the kitchens of fellow dog lovers, adding to the symphony of shared experiences that make our canine companions an integral part of our lives.

Happy cooking, happy bonding, and happy tails!

BONUS MEAL PLANNER

Week: _____

Weekly Meal Planner

Sunday	Monday

Tuesday	Wednesday

Thursday	Friday

Saturday	Notes

Week: _____

Weekly Meal Planner

Sunday	Monday

Tuesday	Wednesday

Thursday	Friday

Saturday	Notes

Week: _____

Weekly Meal Planner

Sunday	Monday

Tuesday	Wednesday

Thursday	Friday

Saturday	Notes

Week: _____

Weekly Meal Planner

Sunday	Monday

Tuesday	Wednesday

Thursday	Friday

Saturday	Notes

Week: _____

Weekly Meal Planner

Sunday	Monday

Tuesday	Wednesday

Thursday	Friday

Saturday	Notes

Week: _____

Weekly Meal Planner

Sunday	Monday

Tuesday	Wednesday

Thursday	Friday

Saturday	Notes
	_____
	_____
	_____
	_____
	_____

69 SLOW COOKER DOG FOOD COOKBOOK

Week: _____

Weekly Meal Planner

Sunday	Monday

Tuesday	Wednesday

Thursday	Friday

Saturday	Notes

Week: _____

Weekly Meal Planner

Sunday	Monday

Tuesday	Wednesday

Thursday	Friday

Saturday	Notes

Week: _____

Weekly Meal Planner

Sunday	Monday

Tuesday	Wednesday

Thursday	Friday

Saturday	Notes

Week: _____

Weekly Meal Planner

Sunday

Monday

Tuesday

Wednesday

Thursday

Friday

Saturday

Notes

_____
_____
_____
_____
_____

Week: _____

Weekly Meal Planner

Sunday	Monday

Tuesday	Wednesday

Thursday	Friday

Saturday	Notes
	_____
	_____
	_____
	_____
	_____

Week: _____

Weekly Meal Planner

Sunday	Monday

Tuesday	Wednesday

Thursday	Friday

Saturday	Notes

75 SLOW COOKER DOG FOOD COOKBOOK

Week: _____

Weekly Meal Planner

Sunday	Monday

Tuesday	Wednesday

Thursday	Friday

Saturday	Notes

Week: _____

Weekly Meal Planner

Sunday

Monday

Tuesday

Wednesday

Thursday

Friday

Saturday

Notes

_____
_____
_____
_____
_____

77 SLOW COOKER DOG FOOD COOKBOOK

Week: _____

Weekly Meal Planner

Sunday	Monday

Tuesday	Wednesday

Thursday	Friday

Saturday	Notes

Week: _____

Weekly Meal Planner

Sunday	Monday

Tuesday	Wednesday

Thursday	Friday

Saturday	Notes

Week: _____

Weekly Meal Planner

Sunday

Monday

Tuesday

Wednesday

Thursday

Friday

Saturday

Notes

_____
_____
_____
_____
_____

Week: _____

Weekly Meal Planner

Sunday	Monday

Tuesday	Wednesday

Thursday	Friday

Saturday	Notes

Week: _____

Weekly Meal Planner

Sunday	Monday

Tuesday	Wednesday

Thursday	Friday

Saturday	Notes

Week: _____

Weekly Meal Planner

Sunday	Monday

Tuesday	Wednesday

Thursday	Friday

Saturday	Notes

Made in the USA
Middletown, DE
07 November 2023

42146195R00046